THE PORCINE CANTICLES

1984 : PORT TOWNSEND

The Porcine Canticles

POEMS BY

David Lee

COPPER CANYON PRESS

Grateful acknowledgment is made to the following periodicals
and anthologies in which some of these poems first appeared:
*Cat's Eye, Chowder Review, The Dragonfly, Kayak, Midwest
Quarterly, Moondance, The Oregon Horseman, Rocky
Mountain Review, Seven Poets, Silver Vain, Soundings,
The Southwest: A Contemporary Anthology, Spoor, Tailwind,*
and *Willow Springs.*

"The Real Estate" is for Herbert Scott and "Day's Work:" the
Ellis Britton poems are for Chant & Ruth, with love.

Publication of this book is made possible in part by a grant
from the National Endowment for the Arts, a federal agency.
Copper Canyon Press is in residence at Centrum.

The type is Sabon, set by Irish Setter
The pig drawings are by Dana Wylder

Copper Canyon Press, Box 271, Port Townsend, WA 98368

FOR JAN, WITH LOVE

Contents

5   Loading a Boar

6   Behold

7   Jubilate Agno

11 Salvage Grain

13 Barbed Wire

17 The Pig Hunt

22 The Hay Swather

25 Building Pigpens

31 Tuesday Morning, Loading Pigs

33 Tuesday Morning,
    Driving to the Auction in Salina

35 The Tale of the Graveblaster

36 The Chain Letter

45 Racehogs

47 The Muffler and the Law

56 Plowing

58 Digging Postholes

62 For Jan, With Love

66 Kolob at Evening

67 Culture

68 Nighthunting with John

70 The Real Estate

75 Fall

76 Jan's Birthday

78 Shoveling Rolled Barley

81 Mean

89 A Day of Mourning, 24 November 75

90 Friday Afternoon, Feeding Pigs

95 Dusk

96 Building a Farrowing Pen

100 The Farm

101 Aftermath

102 Baalam

106 Epilogue

THE PORCINE CANTICLES

Loading a Boar

We were loading a boar, a goddam mean big sonofabitch and he jumped out of the pickup four times and tore out my stockracks and rooted me in the stomach and I fell down and he bit John on the knee and he thought it was broken and so did I and the boar stood over in the far corner of the pen and watched us and John and I just sat there tired and Jan laughed and brought us a beer and I said, "John it ain't worth it, nothing's going right and I'm feeling half dead and haven't wrote a poem in ages and I'm ready to quit it all," and John said, "shit young feller, you ain't got started yet and the reason's cause you trying to do it outside yourself and ain't looking in and if you wanna by god write pomes you gotta write pomes about what you know and not about the rest and you can write about pigs and that boar and Jan and you and me and the rest and there ain't no way you're gonna quit," and we drank beer and smoked, all three of us, and finally loaded that mean bastard and drove home and unloaded him and he bit me again and I went in the house and got out my paper and pencils and started writing and found out John he was right.

Behold

And came forth like Venus from an ocean of
heat waves, morning in his pockets and the buckets in his hands
he emerged from the grey shed, tobacco and wind
pursed together in song from his tight lips he gathered day
and went out to cast wheat before swine. And in
his mind he sang songs and thought thoughts, images of clay
and heat, wind and sweat, dreams of silver and
visions of green earth twisting the cups of his mind
he crossed his fence of wire, the south Utah steppes
bending the air into corners of sky he entered
the yard to feed his swine. And his pigs, they come.

Jubilate Agno

CHRISTOPHER SMART,
1722–1770
IN MEMORIAM

For I will consider my black sow Blackula.

For she is the servant of the god of the feed bucket and serveth him.

For she worships the god in him and the secret of his pail in her way.

For this is done by screams of incantation at the appointed hour and lusty bites of daily communion.

For she stands with forelegs upon the top rail of the wooden fence in supplication.

For she grunts her thanks while she eats.

For she stands for the red boar with closed eyes at the appointed hour.

For having done she lies in mud to consider herself.

For this she performs in ten degrees.

For first she rolls in her wallow to cover her body.

For secondly she lies still to feel the wet.

For thirdly she stretches her length and casts her belly to the sun.

For fourthly she exhales God's air in huge sighs.

For fifthly she rises and examines her feed trough that replenishment might miraculously appear.

For sixthly she scratches her side against the fence.

For seventhly she scratches her jowl with delicate pastern swipe.

For eighthly she smells the breeze to ascertain the red boar's presence.

For ninthly she returns to her mud and plows large holes in the earth.

For tenthly she lies again in the wallow to cool her frame.

For having considered her world she will sleep and dream dreams of herself and her god and the red boar.

For like Eve for softness she and sweet attractive Grace was formed.

For the red boar lusteth mightily and foameth at the mouth for her.

For he might escape and enter her pen.

For if he does this in a non-appointed hour she will scream loudly and
    discourage his kisses.
For her belly is full and needeth no more.
For in one month she will bring forth life in abundance.
For in her last litter she farrowed eight piglets of the red boar.
For three were black and five were red.
For she raised them all and lay on none.
For one in eight is normally crushed by the sow.
For she is exceedingly good in all that she does.
For she is surely of the tribe of Elephant and forgetteth not.
For she weighs near six hundred pounds.
For she has ears of tremendous size.
For she is heavy.
For a large sow is a term of the Titan Elephant.
For she has the appetite of a bird and would eat the day long which in debt
    her master suppresses.
For he would not have her too fat nor his checkbook hollow.
For he keeps her well-fed and she breaks no fence.
For she grunts in pleasure from the mud when he scratches her ears.
For she is a tool of God to temper his mind.
For when she eats her corn she turns and shits in her trough.
For her master is provoked but hereby learns patience.
For she is an instrument for him to learn bankruptcy upon.
For he lost but four dollars each on the last litter of pigs.
For this is admirable in the world of the bank.
For every man is incomplete without one serious debt or loss.
For she provides this with her good faith.
For every farm is a skeleton without a mortgage.
For the Lord admonished black sows when He said lay up no stores of
    treasure on earth.
For she prohibits this daily.
For she is a true child of God and creature of the universe.
For she is called Blackula which is a derivative of the Devil, but false.
For she does worship her God and Savior.
For she was given her name for breaking a fence and eating Jan's garden
    beets.
For when Jan came with a stick and wrath she lifted her head and smiled.

For her teeth and mouth were stained with red beet pulp.
For Jan dropped the stick and laughed.
For she looked like a six-hundred-pound vampire.
For she was called Blackula.
For we feed her red beets daily to watch her smile.
For she is humble when well-fed.
For she makes her point well when she is hungry.
For there is nothing swifter than a sow breaking fence when she desires.
For there is nothing more beautiful than a sow in full run when being chased
    through a garden.
For there is no sound more pure than her scream when she is hit with a stick.
For she is meek in all aspects when satisfied.
For when John Sims saw her lying in mud he proclaimed her majesty.
For he whistled and called her a pretty sonofabitch.
For he offered to trade his beat-up truck for her straight across.
For she has divine spirit and is manifest as a complete pig.
For she is tame and can be taught.
For she can run and walk and sleep and drink and eat.
For she can scream at the red boar.
For she allows her ears and belly to be scratched.
For she allows small children to ride her back.
For she sleeps in mounds of straw at night.
For she produces litters of healthy black and red pigs.
For she can root the earth.
For she can carry sticks in her mouth.
For she will grunt when she is addressed.
For she can jump not far but hard.
For dried earth cracks in the places where she walks.
For she is hated by the breeders of cattle and sheep.
For the former loses more money than I do on his stock.
For the latter fears her mind.
For she has no wool and will not blindly follow his steps.
For he carries no bucket of feed.
For she litters twice per year.
For he litters but once.
For her belly is firm and can take much abuse.
For from this proceeds her worth.

For I perceive God's mystery by stroking her teats.

For I felt tiny lumps of flesh within and knew they were alive.

For the life is the physical substance which God sends from Heaven to sustain the appetites of men.

For God has blessed her womb and the red boar's seed.

For they multiply in ecstasy at the appointed time.

For God has blessed her in many ways.

For God has given her the red beets to eat.

For God has given the water for her to drink.

For God has allowed the water to spill on the ground.

For God allowed the water to turn to mud in a place for her to lay.

For she cannot fly to the mountain streams, though she walks well upon the earth.

For she walks the earth heavy upon tiny feet.

For she treads all the rows of the summer garden.

For she can jump the fence.

For she can push it down.

For she can eat.

Salvage Grain

1

On the way to the feedstore
John sez we oughta be able to get the grain
for two dollars and so when the man bid
two and a quarter I sez that's that
and John moves behind Jan and whispers
bid two thirty and I sez what?
and he winks and I bid and the man bid
two and a half and John calls him a sonofabitch
to Jan and the other man looks at me
to see if I'll bid and I shake my head no
and John he punches me and sez three
and I sez what? and he sez three
and I sez three and the man calls me
a sonofabitch to his wife and the other man sez
what's your name and John sez tell him Homer
and I sez what? and John winks again and I sez
Homer Melvin because that's all I can think
and he tells the secretary to put down Homer
for ten tons and we go home.

2

A month later the man calls John
and sez where's Homer Melvin? and John sez
oh him? he died and the man sez but
he bought all this grain and what am I going to do

and John sez damn he's sorry he don't know
but he'd take it off his hands for two dollars
a hundred and the man sez no and hangs up
but calls John back in an hour and sez
come get it and John calls me
and I get Jan to write a check for two hundred
for our half and we go to meet John to go
to the feedstore and the man looks at me funny
and sez what's your name and I say Dave
and he sez isatso? and John sez you damn right
he's Dave what'd you think I made him
my partner for? and we load our two dollar
grain in John's and my truck and go home.

Barbed Wire

YOU JUST CUT THAT SOMBITCH
RIGHT HERE
      Karl Kopp,
      Yarbrough Mountain

It isn't no easy way
to find the endpiece of wore
onct it's in the roll
you can pick it up bounced it round
like this or roll it
upside the barn hard
mebbe it'll pop out
most times not
don't cost nothing to try
it was this man back home
name Johnny Ray Johnston
a inventer
he invented this thing it could help
find the endpiece
and sent it off to Warshington

he had this brother
name Haroldwayne Johnston
a blind gospel preacher
he wasn't always
he's a mean sonofabitch young
all filt up with sin and equity
fighting raising hell
had three four of them girls
his age up to the doctor
all before he's called
it was this other brother
name Leonas Timothy Johnston

13

he never learnt to read
so he got a job with the highway patrol
got shot by a shiner
I seen that worefinder
it worked my brother he bought one
where'd them pliers go?
so Haroldwayne one day
he's out in this field
where the neighbors run his hogs
hiding in the shinery
shooting a pellet gun
to watch them squolt and run
I guess he was lessee
it was two years before he tried to heal
Mavis Tittle's one that died
of the toothache so he must of been twenty-four
goddam watch it
worell tear the hide right off
your hands you seen them gloves?

this storm come up a sudden
caught him out there
looking like a cyclone
he had to get home so he run
by the time he got to the fence
it was hailballs coming down
he tried to climb through with the gun
poached hisself
shot right up his nose
made all the blood go in his eyeballs
he's blind
that fence caught him
he's straddled of one wore
the top one had him grapt by the butt
here comes the storm
he sez he could feel that wore
go green when the lightening struct

made him a eunuch
he could look right at a naked womern
wouldn't nothing go down
nor come up after that
you find them pliers? look
in the jockey box or under the seat
sez he heard God call him

he'd been hollering like a sonofabitch
they heard all the way to the house
and was fixing to come but he quit
they waited till it quit raining
sez they'd of thought he's dead
and that would of made two
only one brother left for a seed crop
all that blood out his nose
except he's praying to hisself out loud
he never even heard them come up
it isn't none there? look
in the back see if it's some sidecutters
or something so they known he'd got religion
and they never seen he's even blind yet

he's a gospel preacher after
and Johnny Ray's a inventer
Leonas Timothy was arredy shot dead
what it was was a piece of wore
it could be fixed on the end at the store
except it was red paint on it
wherever the red was was the end
when you's through using wore
then fix the red one on
next time there'd be the endpiece red
Haroldwayne he saved hundreds of lostsouls
come all over to hear him heal
best on headaches and biliousness
it was one family had this crippled boy

come about eighty miles to see him gospel preach
brung this boy up front
he taken and grapt his head
hollers the words and sez now walk
but he fell on his ast still crippled
they sez it wasn't Haroldwayne's fault
them people didn't have faith
I heard he drownt a year or two after that

the govament never did send Johnny Ray
no patent agreement we figgered
he kept the invention for hisself
so Johnny Ray he made some up
and sold to his friends around town
you caint buy it nowhere else
I wisht I had one now
I've waste more damn time on wore today
than I have to lose
bring them pliers here
let's cut this sonofabitch it don't matter where
we gone set here all day
won't never get this damn fence done

The Pig Hunt

AFTER READING AN ARTICLE IN PETERSEN'S
Hunting, JANUARY, 1975

I

What if you get caught without a season? Nothing.
Don't despair. Try a farmer. Try a chicken. Old hens,
young layers, some will even fly and can be taken on the wing.
Or a duck. They limp when they walk and this provides more sport
in an unsteady target. Or for the more serious, the mature,
the elite, the by-God-American-sportsMAN there's pigs.
I mean find a farmer, a real down-to-earth, grinning
illiterate, sweaty son-of-a-bitch dirt farmer who raises pigs,
preferably cross-bred spotted variety (spots show up well in
photographs) (spotted pig hides make beautiful rugs) (spots
make wonderful targets). Pay him market price for a hog—
boars are the bargain, at least ten cents a pound below top
market swine, and there is danger in tusks and balls and foam
and boars generally do not move swiftly and make nice stationary
prey for the hunter – and give him five for his trouble,
there's no license anyway so you're still ahead. Have him turn
the beast out of his pen into the field. A corn field is nice,
good concealment, straight rows to sight down, he will browse
while you stalk. Or sagebrush is better. He can hide,
you can hide, the farmer can hide and watch, and your wife's brother
can hide and follow with the Kodak while you hunt the boar.
Use a bow. A rifle is too swift, too easy. A bow is right.
Stalk him quietly, creep close through the forage, wear
your camouflage suit, stay downwind and keep the sun in his eyes,
remember this animal is dangerous, never walk between him
and the feed trough or he may charge. Close in,

17

sight carefully, place the arrow behind his front leg
to catch the lungs and heart. Have a second ready,
he has strength and may run or attack or squeal if wounded.
Pull a full arrow length, feel the surge of power as you peer
down the length of your shaft, tighten your lips as the smooth death
prepares to take wing, release the string and listen
as the behemoth screams in anguish, shoot again as he attempts to rise
and escape, sing as the beast yields to your triumph,
the song of songs, *to eat, to live, to hunt, this is life*, glory
in the red foam spreading the earth, secure in your fame
for you have toed the mark once more and again are affirmed as Man.

2

            "I couldn't believe him
            he sez I'll buy your hog
            and I sez you don't raise hogs
            and he sez I know
            but I'll buy yours
            and I sez sixty dollars
            and he nods good and gives me
            sixty five and sez let him out
            and that silly shitass chases him
            down the field with a bow
            and arrow until the hog stops
            to eat some alfalfa
            and he gets down on his belly
            crawls close and shoots and
            shoots and shoots and the hog
            goes down he yells
            and his brother-in-law comes up
            takes his picture with the dead hog
            arrows sticking out all over
            and he keeps saying
            by God I put him away didn't I?"

18

3

"The art is in the lens.
An idiot can aim and press
the button, the artist focuses the moment.
Eternity. The action of the chase
as they run through tangled sage,
the saga of life and death
stalking each other
a glimpse of sunlight filling
old paths as they meet
captured forever in the exposed film
man and boar and artist."

4

"Pig, I hunted you in the old ways
stalked you as I did once
long ago before the concrete and asphalt
before they put you in small pens
to breed away your spirit and soul.

Pig, in death I gave you life
the moment of truth when we stood
face to face again as it was
and should be, when you saw your death
and knew and stood in majesty, unafraid.

Pig, now we share the eternal bond
of brotherhood, your blood mingled
in mine throbbing the years
until we rise to meet again in perfection
and know forever the ecstasy of the hunt.

Pig, sleep well. Gather your dreams
for the day when we become one."

5

"I don't mind the picture on the wall,
men gather trophies to spell their lives
as corners gather dust and memory.

I don't mind Jim's signature in the corner
or the sign Don made, 'note the short
but sharp tusks beneath the monster's lip.'

I don't mind hearing the endless tales
of brotherhood and freedom and communion
every night in the dining room.

What I do mind is the bristles spreading
across the floor, plugging my vacuum
each time he walks across his rug.

What I do mind is the kids
bringing in their friends from school
to see the big pig Daddy shot.

What I do mind is the questions
I'm asked by my friends, the sly smiles,
the time I heard Joan call me Mrs. Hogslayer.

That I mind a lot."

6

We were building fence
and it was hot. John strung
and stretched and I followed, hammering
steeples. He worked and I worked
and we both sweat a lot.
John, I said finally when I got tired,
I read in this magazine about farmers

renting out their hogs to hunters.
John didn't say anything so I went on,
they let hunters come in and hunt
their hogs. I mean, I said, the hunters
come in and pay them market price
and a little for their trouble
to hunt their pigs in their fields
with a bow and arrow.

John didn't turn but went on working
so I worked some more
until I caught up to him
ready to say reckon you ought to do that
because John would say something
and I'd laugh because it would
be funny. John puts down the roll of fence
before I talk and sits on it
then John says, I seen that book
that ignorant goddam book
and I'd like to find the man
who shot that pig and the farmer
and the bow and arrow
the whole goddam mess and lock them
in a room with the dead hog
and let them stay there forever
that's what I'd do.
What kind of a goddam man would even think
of something like that?
And he started working again
and I worked
and we built the fence
and I was glad I hadn't said anything
about hunting John's pigs.

The Hay Swather

Dave John sez Dave is that you?
I sed hello John
John sez it's that damn swoker I bought
I sed did something go wrong arredy?
John sez yas so I sed but you just got it
it shouldn't break down that quick
was it bad? Goddam John sez
it busted all to hell
the manifold bushings mebbe a flywheel bearing
it could of been the drive shaft or cam I dunno
I tried to fix it and climbed underneath and beat it
with the hammer so when I went to start it up
the clutch jerked a knot in hisself
and felt across the ground
I had a hundred more acres of hay I told him
I'd knock down before weekend
and I didn't even have a dog with me
to kick his ast
it wasn't nothing I could do but stand and watch

I sed John I don't know anything
about machinery John sez whar?
I sed nowhere
John sez oh well that don't matter now
so I sed that's good
John sez if I could of found him I'd of
loosen up his hide right now
I sed whose? John sez

the one that solt me the swoker who you talking about?
I sed oh him
John sez yas but it was too late
sos I went home and made up these words
I practiced what to say in the night
next morning I got my truck and drove
to the crossroads before I got there I stopped
and put some of the words on my hand
sos I wouldn't be lost when I got mad
and if I hit him I'd have them all right there
he'd know how come
cause he was gone say well John I be damn
I'm sorry but it was a used one and all
there ain't nothing he can do

I pulled up and he's standing right there
eating a sandwich for breakfast
and sez hello John I sez I gotta talk to you
right now he sez you want a sandwich
he hadn't had his breakfast yet
I sez no I ain't got no time to eat a sandwich
I'd eat a cupcake and a can of viennies
on the way so he sez come in
we went in his office and set down
I lain my hand out on the table sos I could
see the words I sez listen here
that swoker you solt me done busted all to hell
and it ain't been that long
and you ought to do something about it
it ain't right that way
I didn't say or I'll whup your ast
but I had it wrote down
if I needed it for later

he didn't say nothing
he picked up the phone I thot he's calling

the law mebbe but he sez Roy
tell Bubba unload that big truck to somebody
and he sez yeah now
I'll need it this morning sos he hangs up
the phone he sez John well
it's only one thing I can do
we'll go load up my swoker and take it out
to your place sos you won't lose no time
and load yours up and I'll bring it back
and fix her up cause I guarantee it
all I sell for ninety days
if it busted reckon it's my fault not yours
so what else can I do for you this morning?

I sed John what'd you say?
John sez I looked at my hand
and I ain't wrote nothing for that
so I sez that sandwich sounds fine
it's all I could think of
and I wasn't even hungry
I couldn't shake his hand
cause he might see them words I put on it
I never thought he'd go and say
something like that
and I couldn't just set there
so he torn his in half and we both
eat a piece waiting

Building Pigpens

meanest man ever
was Ellis Britton
I known of him for years
before I known who he was
I went to school with his boy Melvin
we called him swamprat
he's half cross-eyed couldn't help it
he got killed in the war jumping out airplanes in Franct
he flown all over the world in the army
before he got killed they sed
is it a longboard over there anywheres?
we can put a longboard on the bottom rail
to stop digging out mebbe
so onct he was driving along in his car
he seen this man building a pigpen
he's doing the front fence
and it was this level he was using
to get it straight because
it was beside his house
you could see it from the road
he wanted it to look nice he sez
Ellis Britton he stopped his car
rolt down his winder
and sez what in hell are you doing?
you don't use no goddam level to build
no pigpen you stop that
that man he waved Ellis Britton drove off
that night taken and come back

he torn that pigpen apart
right to the ground with a crowbar
sez he couldn't stand it no more
to put on no airs that way
hand me them nails in the sack
them sixteen pennies

he raised hogs for awhile
couldn't stay in the business
he killed his boar one day
this sow was posta be in
he put the boar to her but she
wasn't ready that boar he
didn't want to wait round
got excited cut her side open
with his tuskies
god it made Ellis Britton mad
he run in his house got his gun
come back he shot that boar
in the head but it was a 22
the boar was old had a thick bone
it never killed him at first
he run off squolling
Ellis Britton he chased him down
shot up a whole shirtpocket
full of bullets killing that boar
cut this board off where I marked it
with the nail right there see?
he killed two other pigs
and shot four more other ones
that never died
when the boar went down
he busted the 22 acrost his head
and he'd give it to his boy
for a Christmas present
it wasn't even his

he was deer hunting this time
and it was this horse
he'd borrowed from his wife's brother
so he shot this deer
tried to load it on the horse
they's a long ways out
that horse didn't want to carry that deer
he hadn't done that before
so Ellis Britton tried to load him
but he shied
goddam you cut the wrong mark
I sed the one I marked with the nail
where's that board?
you done ruint it find me anothern
so he give it three tries
then he got his gun
shot that horse and walked home
his wife had to call her brother
and tell him so he could go get
his saddle off the dead horse
if he wanted it
how about that one over there
the long one will it work?

had to put him in jail onct
it was this boy rode his motorsickle
at night Ellis Britton he was sleeping
he rode it by his house on the road
out front riding round these blocks
he went by a few times
woken Ellis Britton up he couldn't
go back to sleep so he got up
went out in his shed and got his rope
he tied it to these two trees
where it went acrost the road so
here come this boy
it's not long enough

is it one any longer out there?
look in that pile over there
he hit that rope right on his shoulders
busted out both collerbones
they sez if it'd of been a inch higher
it'd of tore his head off
and broke his neck
soon as he hit Ellis Britton run out
in the street he taken out his knife
and cut holes in both motorsickle tores
he went back in his house
never even called the ambulance
neighbors had to when they heard that boy
screaming Ellis Britton went to bed
bring that one over here
I think it'll be long enough
they arrested him and put him in jail
so next morning
Charley Baker's daughter she was a idiot
her tongue stuck out her mouth all day
slobbered down the front her dress
she brought these breakfast
it was scrambled eggs with applesauce
on top of it she'd fixed
and slud it in his cell
she set down to watch him eat it
like she always did
you couldn't stand to eat with her
setting there slobbering at you
so most prisoners they'd just slud it back
she'd eat it right in front of them
with her fingers
it was puke all over that jailhouse
after breakfast some days
she could remember and find the ketchup
can you cut this one right?
follow the mark right there

28

don't cut it half in two this time
Ellis Britton he set right down in front of her
on the other side the bars
he eat the whole thing with his hands
her setting there watching
when he's done he used his fingers
sopped up the rest
he slud the plate back so she picked it up
and looked at it then she
turnt it up and licked this one spot
Ellis Britton he jumped up
he reached his arm through the bars
grapt that plate he sez
goddam is it some more on there?
that's mine you caint have it
Charley Baker's daughter she hollered
like hell she run off
wouldn't bring him nothing else
they let him go that afternoon

so he got this job as a conductor
and ticket taker on the railroad
he damn near ruint that whole run
it was to whar it was a line
ever Thursday and Saturday
to take the Greyhound bus
nobody would ride the train
see I knew you could do it
if you'd pay attention
that education has to be
worth something you'd think
they sez some folks would go on
to the next town twelve mile away
and ride the bus back or hitch
just so they wouldn't have to have
Ellis Britton help them get off the train
and find their suitcase

29

he was so mean
how come you just standing there?
find another board
we here to work
not just set round wasting time
so then it was this other time he taken and

Tuesday Morning,
Loading Pigs

The worse goddam job of all
sez John pushing a thick slat
in front of the posts
behind the sow in the loading chute
so when she balked and backed up
she couldn't turn and get away
I never seen a sow or a hog load easy
some boars will
mebbe it's because they got balls
or something I don't know
but I seen them do it
that Brown feller the FFA
he's got this boar he just opens the trailer door
he comes and gets in
course he mebbe knows what
he's being loaded up for

it was this Ivie boy back home
the best I ever seen for loading
he wasn't scared of nothing
he'd get right in and shove them up
he put sixteen top hogs
in the back of a Studebaker pickup
by hisself I seen it
when he was a boy he opened up
the tank on the tractor
smelling gas
made his brains go soft they sed

he failed fifth grade
but it wasn't his fault
he could load up hogs

I always had to at home
cause I was the youngest
I sed then it was two things
I wouldn't do when I grown up
warsh no dishes or load up hogs
by god they can set in the sink
a month before I'll warsh them
a man's got to have a principle
he can live by is what I say
now you grab her ears and pull
I'll push from back here
we'll get that sonofabitch in the truck

Tuesday Morning,
Driving to the Auction in Salina

Sometimes sez John
it's so pretty here I caint stand it
I'm on that hay swoker
it's green alfalfa all in front
and then them red Utah hills behind
climb up to the mountains
just like they're pasted on blue

but then it's times I'm alone I listen past it all
I hear Misippi
like a big muscle holding its blood
and the slosh on them rotten piles
down behind the house at night
I can almost see
that moon trying to push up the sky
reflected off the water
and the clouds fall apart
like pieces of paint
coming off old walls in the bedroom
it's almost the taste of fog
floating down the river
behind the cold nightwind
you know what I mean?

and John drove in silence
thinking me asleep
as I stared out toward the shrouded river

a thousand miles distant
listened to the sliding brown water
move over the etched memory
of a red and white bobber
dancing on the ripples of my mind

The Tale of the Graveblaster

On the way to the auction in Salina to sell our pigs John told a story about a graveblaster he knew in Pioche. Not a digger, the ground was too hard so he had to blast his graves out with dynamite. John couldn't remember the man's name but he had a son named Manuel who the story was about anyway. There was a day when the father was ill and had to be taken to the hospital in Ely. Afternoon, the mortician called and asked for the father; only Manuel was left to blast the grave. He loaded his father's truck with the sticks from the case, fused the charge, walked behind a small knoll and detonated the explosives. The blast carved a huge gap in the earth which spread much farther than Manuel had anticipated. Nearby graves were upthrust and several coffins disinterred and scattered profusely about the area. John's story struck me as being somewhat sardonically humorous and I laughed. Incredulous, John slowed his truck, cut me off with a glance. "It ain't funny you sonofabitch," he said. "That was his daddy's grave he was blasting."

The Chain Letter
(An American Tragedy)

Ohdammit sez John I'm in trouble
so I sed why John?
John sez I got the bill for my insurance
and I haven't got no money to pay it
cause I won't get paid for swoking and bailing
Keith Guymon's hay till next week
I done told him that would be just fine
when he ast a week ago but
LaVerne she went and opened the damn envelope
on a chain letter and I ain't got no time
to write out twenty copies
I got to get that hay finished
so what am I posta do now?

I sez what John? John sez
it's the damn govament
sends them things out I know it
and it works with the post office and
the insurance to keep you in line
I sez what John?

John sez my brother onct
he got this chain letter back home
he didn't have no time
to write out his copies neither
it sez he has four days to wrote it
before the luck comes good or bad
it ain't never good I heard of

but he forgot
back then it was $5,000 this feller got
in four days and then later
when the govament ruint the money
he put on a zero it was $50,000
and then it was $100,000
now it sez he got $420,000
it's the same guy it was in
that letter back then
just the numbers changed
it's the way the govament has
to let us know how much
he's gone let the money be worth
but the next day because he hadn't
wrote out his twenty letters
he lost all that money
but my brother he was busy too
he didn't do his letters

the third day after
he had to go kill these pigs
for this man but this other feller
was gone bring his milkcow down
get her bred to my brother's bull
he told him go ahead and do it
he sez he'd have his boy
walk her down the road
it wasn't far
so while my brother was gone
his boy brought her down
turnt her in the corral
he climbt up on the fence to watch

it might of been fine
except the hogs been rooting
up under the barn wall
my brother he borrowed

this lectric fence
he strung it along the side of the barn
so the bull mounts up on the milkcow
she turns and backs him up
against the barn he's stuckt
he gets his back feet
tangled in that lectric fence
one in front and one back
he tries to move and he just tightens
up the lectric wire
that boy he sez you could hear it
zzip zzip zipp that bull
he starts to bellering
milkcow she don't know
what's going on so she backs him up
tighter against the barn
it isn't no way he can get off
he commences to jumping up and down
on her and trying to get his feet
loost of that lectric wire
but he caint it goes zzip
he bellers and she backs up more
it goes zzip again
it was like he was doing a dance
like them crazy people do
trying to get his legs loost
hollering like a sonofabitch

so it was hogs there too
they heard it and here they come
it wasn't natural and a hog
it won't let nothing that's not natural
stay that way around them
it has to get right or go away or die
that boy sez they all run up
grunted and squolt like hell
when that didn't work

this one old mean bitching sow
she run right in between them
she bit that bull right on his seeds
she wanted him to stop acting that way
making all that noise
jumping up and down like that
right now

that bull he just went over backwards
right up against the barn
like he'd been shot in the head
knocked the whole goddam end
of the barn down
fell right on his back
the end rafter come down
on his chest it torn a piece of skin off
his pecker to his seeds
wide as your hand
they swolt up like basketballs
from the hogbite
broke ribs they figured
but it never did kill him
that milkcow she wasn't finished
she kept backing up
and fell down right on top of him
it was only the end of the barn
come down the rest stood up
that boy he's scairt
he got his daddy's milkcow up
off my brother's bull he left
he sed he seen enough for onct

my brother that night
he's coming home from killing them hogs
he never knew none of this happened yet
he's driving see? and he'd lost
his picking finger on his left hand

in the leaf springs of a wagon
when we's kids so
he's driving left-handed
and doing the gears and picking
with his right hand
it was a moon out so he'd turned off
his pickup lights listening
to the radio because his battery
wasn't much good
he couldn't do both
while he was driving
he couldn't see good as
he thought he could
he hit this big chuckhole
slung him right into the steering wheel
he figured it would of broke his nose
if he hadn't been picking
but his hand took the cushion
it only give him a nosebleed
but almost broke his hand
where it hit
his knuckles was bruised so bad
he couldn't even open and shut
his fingers for a week
he had to drive the rest of the way home
left-handed and lean acrost
and shift with that hand too
he thought the other one was broke
but it wasn't

he got home and the first thing
he seen was the end of his barn out
that bull standing there
inside the barn with his head down low
my brother thought he'd butted it down
he run in the house to get his gun
he was mad he would of kilt that bull

40

but they told him how it happened
so he didn't
he went out to look
but it wasn't no way they could
get that bull to go back in that yard
where them pigs was
he wouldn't go out the barn
they hit him acrost the butt
with a board he'd just stand there
he didn't care no more

they went in the house
my brother he got out the dishpan
and soaked some cold water
so he lain his hand in it
to get the swollen to go down
he wouldn't tell them how it happened
at first but while he was setting there
with his hand ducked
he remembered that chain letter
he jumped up and run to get it
sloshed water all over the kitchen floor
he was hollering how long's it been?
how long's it been?
they sez it happened this morning
it was just this morning
he sez whar? they sez when the sow
bit the bull on his seeds
knocked the barn down
he hollers no not that
how long's it been since I got
this here chain letter in the mail?
they sez oh three days
he sez goddam I only got one day left

my brother he set up all night
writing out his twenty copies

he had to tape the pencil to his hand
cause it was swole up
his fingers wouldn't bent
they sed he even wrote some
with his left hand
it was so bad you couldn't
read the words
he got them all done by sunup
the fourth day like it sed
and took it to the mailbox

he waited all morning on the porch
till they remembered it was Memoral Day
the mail he wouldn't come
my brother he about had a worm
he run out to the mailbox
and got them letters he run over
to his pickup and clumb in
it wouldn't crunk
he'd run the battery down
listening to the radio
goddam my brother he was mad
he busted the side winder
with his head when that pickup
wouldn't turn over
jumped out and slammed the door
so hard it didn't catch
it bounced back and hit him
right on his swole up hand
it hurt so bad he sez
he nearly fainted of the pain
he knew he had to get them letters
in the mail
so he walked all the way to town
it was moren ten miles back then

it worked
nothing else happened
they got the end back in the barn
without it coming down
but they had to shoot the bull finally
and eat him
because he wouldn't do nothing
just set there and waste away
he'd seen enough they guessed
it wasn't no way he'd go
back out there with them pigs
in the corral

since then ever time
we seen a envelope in my family
it looks like it might be a chain letter
we don't open it till we got time
to set down right then
and make out them twenty copies
like it sez to do
but this time LaVerne must of forgot
it snuck up on her
when I got home it was laying
on the table and it wasn't nothing
I could do
it was my name on the envelope

I know it come from the insurance company
it was two years ago the man's wife
from the insurance called
she sez to LaVerne then that she wanted her
to come to her house
she wanted to tell her about selling Amway
LaVerne she sez she wasn't inarrested
a week later here comes
the insurance bill
by god it's gone up almost double

I sez how come you didn't go?
you could of just set and nod
now see what happened?
but it was too late

so I'm gone have to stay up tonight
writing chain letters
I done wrote one to send to the insurance
so he'll know I did it
and let the govament know
I wrote him a note on the bottom
and sez I'll pay the insurance bill
as soon as I can
but things is tough all over
I just hope he'll understand
I'd as soon right now
rather not have no luck at all
but I am willing to cooperate
if that's what my duty is
as a patriotic American citizen

Racehogs

John calls and sez Dave
when I say hello and I say hello John
and he sez come down Dave
you gotta see what I got
I say fine I'll be right there and he sez
bring Jan I'll show her too
and I said I will
so Jan and I got in the car to see
what John bought.

John bought four hogs
starved half to death, bones out
everywhere, snouts sharp enough
to root pine trees and the longest damn legs
I've seen. What do you think? he sez
and I don't say anything so he sez
I sez what do you think? and I say
them's pretty good-looking racehogs John
and he sez what? and I tell him
I heard about a place in Japan or California
(because he's never been there) where they
have a track and race hogs
on Tuesday nights and he sez do they
pay much? and I say yes or so I heard
maybe a hundred to win and he sez
goddam and I say those hogs
ought to be good with them long legs
and skinny bodies and he sez goddam.

Jan's walked off so I go find her
but she's mad and says I ought not to do that
and I say oh I was just bullshitting
but when we come back John's standing
by the fence throwing little pieces of feed
all around the pen making the hogs
hurry from one place to the next
and when I get up close he's smiling
and I can hear him whisper
while he throws the feed
run you skinny fuckers, run.

The Muffler and the Law

I

You got a sow in heat? John sez
this morning when he called
I sed oh yas John I got four right now
John sez it wouldn't one
be that big black one would it?
I sed yas she's in I'm going to turn her
in with the boar this afternoon
John sez I'll be right down
to get her I want to borrow that sow
he hung up

John brought his beat up truck
to my house with his big spotted boar
loaded in the back and a partition
so another hog could be put in
but the boar couldn't get to it
he drove right out to my loading chute
by the time I got there
John was trying to load up my big black sow
I sed John what are you doing?
John looked at me like I was crazy
he sez you gone hep me or stand there?
I didn't say anything else
I helped John load up my big black sow
and John drove off with her
in his truck and never did say where

47

2

Late afternoon John drove up
to my house he honks
he yells Dave come hep me unload
this big black sow of yours
she's done bred
I don't need her no more
he drives out back
to the loading chute
and unloads the sow
before I can get there

3

John I sed what the hell's going on
I mean you come get my big black sow
drive off without telling me anything
and you bring her back bred
to your spotted boar
what if I didn't want her bred to him?
John sez no charge
so it was all right then
I was going to tell him he could take
the other three sows that were in
for a ride all day tomorrow if he wanted
but John shut the gate on his stock racks
and sat down on his tailgate

it was this deputy sheriff
John sez so I sed which? John sez
that one in Richfield
last week going to the auction at Salina
I run over this rockslide
on the cutoff by Cove Fort
I busted my muffler pipe loost
and all the brackets I had to stop

on the summit and fix it all up
with bailing wire
it took a hour almost and I was late
for the auction so I had to go
the muffler was loost
and it made noise
but I didn't have no more time
I had to hurry

I got to Richfield
here comes this law
his red lights on and his siren honking
right in the middle of town
I got out and sez I'm late to the auction
he slams his car door and put his hand
on it he puts his other hand right down
on his gun sez I don't know whar
YOU from mister but in MY town
we got a law here
I'm standing there with a truckload of hogs
people driving by slow looking at me
right in the middle of Richfield
I sez I'm late to the auction again
what I done wrong this time?
he sez in my town we got a law
against loud mufflers so you gone have
to pay you a fine for it mister
I sez look I done hit this rock slide
coming and busted
I tried to wire it up but couldn't
you look under here you can see
I'm late to the auction
his red lights was still going

I bent down to show him the wire underneath
he jumped in his car and taken out
his microphone he called this other law

so I stood up he sez you stand right there
I sez whar ? he sez right there
he jumps out his car and puts his hand
on his gun again sez you trying
to resist arrest on me
I sez no I'm trying to show you
the bailing wire under here
holding up the pipes and the muffler
where I hit the rock on the mountain
but I caint hold the muffler on right
and the auction starts in fifteen minutes
he sez you just stand right there still
I got a reaforcement coming
we gone arrest you

4

I sed what happened John ? John
sez the other law he come
and they both wrote me out a ticket
for loud mufflers and resisting arrest
and the other one that come
sez he believed I was speeding too
but they never wrote a ticket for it
and that's too bad cause I was
I was late for the auction

I sez can I go now ? but the law
he sez you got to pay your fine
I sez the auction started five minutes ago
and I got to get there
the other law he sez why you
going to the auction you selling hogs ?
I never sez a word to that dumb sonofabitch
he's standing right there by my truck
loaded up with twelve top hogs
wallering each other in the middle of town

all the cars driving by watching
the first law sez you got to foller us
to the J. P. I sez isn't it no other way?
he sez you trying to bribe a officer of law?
I sez hell no I'm trying to get to the auction
the other law sez whar?
and the first sez Salina they sell hogs at one
I sez that was ten minutes ago
the other law sez you selling these hogs?
but I wasn't talking to him
the law sez you want a regular judge
you can come back next Friday
but the fine goes up for that
I sez can I go now? and the law sez yas
but the other one sez not till you
get that muffler fix

I had to get my truck towed
to a filling station four blocks away
and the muffler pipe welted
he charged me forty-seven dollars
and sixty-five cents to do it
I could of done it for a dollar
at home if I had my tools
by then the auction was over
I had to drive all them pigs home
after I'd loaded them up that morning
to take to the auction at Salina

5

I sed that's too bad John
John sez I couldn't sleep about it
for a man to talk to me that way
all he had to done was look
under the truck so he could see

51

it wasn't my fault
I tried to fix it best I could

he sez the fine would go up
so I sez to myself John it's done costed
fifty dollars almost so you
might as well get your say out of it
but I didn't have no sow in heat
so that's how come I called you

I sed John I don't understand
John sez I drove to Richfield
with that panel between the hogs
my spotted boar he about chewed it
in two trying to get your big black sow
but he couldn't so I went right to the spot
where that law pulled me over
in the middle of town
I stopped my truck and got out
climbed up on my stockracks
I took out the panel
let the boar go to her

I sed you did what? John sez
by god she wasn't quite ready yet
she squolt and here come the cars to see
I bet they could hear her half a mile
then here come the law
with his red light on
he sez what in the hell is you doing?
I sez here I am to pay my fine
he sez you get that truck out of here
with them pigs people's watching
I sez whar? he waved his arms he sez
everwhar see them they all coming
I sez I got to pay my fine I come to go
to court he sez whar? I sez right here

lord it was horrible my spotted boar
he slobbered all over your black sow
it was hog slobber on both her ears
that law he's as red in the face
as a fox's ass he couldn't do nothing
he finally sez you get your truck
you foller me I sez that's fine
but go slow I got a load of hogs in mine
I caint be jostling them any
we drove to the courthouse

6

Judge he sez what's going on?
law he sez you honor he's disturbing peace
Judge he sez how? law he sez
he's got these pigs in his truck
and they copperlating in the middle of town
Judge he sez whar? law he sez
right out there so Judge gets up
he looks out his winder there's my truck
by now my spotted boar he's done
he lain down and wasn't getting up
pooped Judge sez all I see is a hog
law he sez but they was scruting!
Judge he sez don't you talk that way
in a court of law you hear me?
all I see is a hog and it isn't no law
that sez this man caint haul no hog
through town in his truck yet
so I sez you honor I want you to listen
to my side of this so I told him
the whole story about the muffler
and the law how I missed the auction
he looks at that law he sez
is it the way it happened like he sez?
law he commenced to squirming

but he has to say yassir you honor finally
I told him how it costed me fifty dollars almost
to get it fix and I had to be towed
four blocks with twelve top hogs in the truck
Judge he sez case dismissed and he sez
to me he's sorry about it all
specially the fifty dollars so I sez it's the way it is
cain't be nothing done now
I didn't have no more hard feelings
so we shaken hands and I left

law he's mad as hell outside waiting
he sez mister you ever come to my town
again I'll make you sweat I'll
arrest your ass and thow you in jail
I sez mister deputy sheriff law
you listen here you listen good
you ever bother me again for anything
next time I'll pull a trailer and bring
eight sows and three boars all together I'll park
in front of the schoolhouse and take out the panel
I'll go in and tell them you sez for me
to meet you there and where are you
you posta have the money for me for them hogs
if you don't believe it you just try
and I sez then so you just get out my way
I walked on past him and went and left
he never sez one more word to me

7

so here's your big black sow
John sed and he stood up
she's done bred to my spotted boar
but you don't owe me nothing
I ain't never won one with the law before
so I reckon this one's on me

54

John closed his tailgate and leaned in
and patted his spotted boar
on the head and then John got in
his beat up truck and drove home for supper

Plowing

1

All my life. Broken ground.
Shovels. John Deere bangers. Sticks, cats, hoes
always forgotten people speak
old ways, lost ways, fossils.

I found an old plow
bought leather straps, borrowed John's
half blind Dan   *n goddamit boy*
don let that sonnybitch kick ya he's mean bastard
sed John, helped me with harness.

2

My anticipations all misplaced,
early plowed under. Expected sun
and flesh, tracings and neck leaders
mind drifting to Kolob's breezes,
tired arms, hoarse throat.

Found wind, thick clods. John's Dan
walked easy, followed his good eye
in straight lines. I moved, something habitual,
behind, stepping over turned earth
shy at harness
precariously balanced on one of the world's edges
wind against my hair
exploding into afternoon   *god aint he sumin*

that mule's so old he carried Moses inta Jewsalem
and he aint forgot a goddam thang
wind and earth and animal
the only geometry.

3

All my life I've heard death
takes us to the cycle's center,
where we should be, crystals
clusters. We exist within, know
both sides at once. Perfect definition.

And that life is broken parabola.
We wander against wind, random circles,
no closer to center, glimpses,
shadows and edges   *I caint tell ya how to do it boy*
its gonna be there in ya bones or it aint shit for nowhere
the world inside. And I followed John's mule
my boots relaxed in stillness, shattered dust

plowed earth, wind, sky.
And John walked beside, talked of hog markets
hollow bones, lakebottoms and forgotten ways.
The moon swallowed dusk. Our image
crystalized against a backdrop of night.

Digging Postholes

was teaching his boy Melvin
how to play some baseball
so he stolt this baseball bat
off the churchhouse softball team
brung it home
he opened up the garage door
a little bit he put these little gravels
down on the ground inside
had Swamprat stand there
ever evening before dark for a week
holding the baseball bat
and the swallers'd come out
they'd see them gravels
flown down to get it
the way they do
so Melvin when they come in
through the door
he'd see them coming in out of the light
he'd swat at them with that bat
learning to hit baseballs
that's deep enough
I done got a cedarpost
youg'n go head and dig the next one
Ellis Britton he'd whup his ast
if he didn't hit some
ever night you could hear him
hollering boy you
keep you eye on the sonofabitching ball

you swinging like a damn girl
you want me to get you a orningboard?

Melvin he'd bawl
he'd squowl I'm trying goddammit
Daddy them bastards won't holt still
Ellis Britton he'd holler
just clost your mouth boy
here comes anothern get ready
where'd that tamping rod go?
so he'd hit a few they's all squashed up
out in front of the garage
here come the cats

Ellis Britton he knew them cats'd
bring him bad luck
if he let them stay around
so he taken and borrowed this pellet gun
from the preacher's boy
made this one daughter of his
set on the porch with the gun
while he heped Swamprat
learn to hit baseballs
and shoot them cats when she seen it
sneaking up on the garage
to get them dead swallers
it was this one she shot at
ripped him a little bit somewhars
that cat couldn't think of nothing to do
but climb a tree
it wasn't no tree out there
just Ellis Britton
he's hollering how'd I ever
get a piss ignorant boy
like you? you done missed anothern
I'm running out of patients boy goddammit
that cat clumb right up him
that one'll be a cornerpost

dig it a little bit deeper okay?
so Ellis Britton
like he got his tit in the wringer
bellers godamitey godamitey
get him off get him offme
Melvin he sez is it one coming Daddy?
his daughter she commenced
to pumping that pellet gun up
hollering Melvin Melvin
that cat went right up the side his face
torn whole handfuls of hair out his head
he couldn't grab it fast enuf
just hollers get him off
get him OFF me
his daughter yells Melvin Leon
Melvin Leon pumps that gun
Ellis Britton's wife comes out the housedoor
screams jesus godamitey judastpriest
Swamprat runs out the garagedoor
he sez whar whar? Ellis Britton hollers
get him off get him off
that cat about torn his ear in two
he grabbed holt and was hanging on
Ellis Britton's wife she hollers
do sumin DO sumin
Melvin he sez whar is it whar is it?
his daughter hollers on his head see him
on his head she shoots Ellis Britton
in the shoulder with the pellet gun
Melvin yells I seen him holt still
Ellis Britton's wife hollers help your daddy
HELP your daddy Ellis Britton he yells
goddam what was that?
when that pellet hit him in his shoulder
he turns round Melvin
he hit him in the face
with the baseball bat

the cat run off and hid
when he fell down
got away

it should be a big cedarpost in the pile
see if you can find one for the corner
so his nose was busted
it broken off half his front teeth
he had them all pult out
got him some storeboughten ones
sez it wasn't worth it to fix them
it costed too much
most was rotten anyways
they had to operate on him
to get that pellet out his shoulder
that cat never did come back

Melvin didn't get picked
for the baseball team that summer
he could hit but he couldn't catch
he had this one eye it was crossed
he couldn't find the ball
up in the air after itus hit
that's a good one bring it over here
they's afraid he'd get his brains knocked out
if it was a flyball hit on his head
they known Ellis Britton
he'd sue the Little League if it did
so they wouldn't let him play no baseball
they couldn't afford it
stick it in and scrape up some dirt
with your foot and I'll get the tamping rod
so then after that he

For Jan,
With Love

I

John he comes to my house
pulls his beat up truck in my drive
and honks
Dave John sez Dave my red sow
she got pigs stuck and my big hands they won't go
and I gotta get them pigs out
or that fucker she's gonna die
and I sez John goddam
we'll be right down and John sez Jan
he yells JAN where's Jan she's got little hands
she can get in there and pull them pigs
and I sez Jan and he sez Jan and Jan comes
what? Jan sez and John sez tell Jan Dave
and I sez Jan John's red sow's got pigs
stuck and his hands too big and won't go
and he's gotta get them pigs out
or that fucker's gonna die (John he turns
his head and lights a cigarette)
(he don't say fuck to no woman)
and Jan she sez well let's go
and we get in John's beat up damn truck
and go to pull John's pigs

2

John's red sow she doesn't weigh
a hundred and sixty pounds
but he bred her to his biggest boar
and had to put hay bales by her sides
so the boar wouldn't break
her back because Carl bet five dollars
he couldn't and John he bet
five she could and John he won
but Carl enjoyed watching anyway

3

John's red sow was laying
on her side hurting bad
and we could see she had a pig
right there but it wouldn't come she
was too small and John sez see
and I sez I see that pig's gotta come out
or that fucker's gonna die
and Jan puts vaseline on her hands
and sez hold her legs and I hold her legs
and Jan goes in after the pig
and John gets out of the pen and goes
somewheres else

Jan she pulls like hell pretty soon
the pig come big damn big little pig
dead and I give Jan more vaseline and she goes
back in to see about any more
and John's red sow pushes hard on Jan's arm
up to her elbow inside and Jan sez
there's more help me and I help
another pig damn big damn dead comes
and John's red sow she seems better
and we hope that's all

4

John's red sow won't go
out of labor so we stay all night
and John brings coffee and smokes
and flashlight batteries and finally Jan
can feel another pig but John's red sow's
swole up tight and she can't grab hold
but only touch so I push her side
and she grunts and screams and shits all over Jan's arm
and Jan sez I got it help me and I help
and we pull for a goddam hour and pull
the pig's head off

and I sez oh my god we gotta get that pig now
or that fucker's gonna die for sure
and John sez what happened? and Jan
gives him a baby pig's head in his hand
and John goes somewheres else again
while Jan goes back fast inside
grabbing hard and John's red sow
hurts bad and Jan sez I got something help me
and I help and we start taking that pig out
piece by piece

5

Goddam you bitch don't you die
Jan yells when John's red sow don't help no more
and we work and the sun comes up
and finally we get the last piece of pig out
and give John's red sow a big shot of penicillin
her ass swole up like a football
but she don't labor and John sez
is that all? and Jan wipes her bloody arms

on a rag and sez yes and John climbs in
the pen and sez how's my red sow?
and we look and go home and go to bed
because John's red sow that fucker she died

Kolob at Evening

I WENT TO THE EDGE OF THE WOOD
IN THE COLOR OF EVENING...
   John Haines

The color of evening washed at my feet
and I dreamed years of dying suns
buried in the west end of Kolob Lake

old fishermen on their grey rocks,
beaver and swallows mating in the eclipse
of twilight and dusk
sink in the splashing reflection
to the meadows beneath the mirror
where fat trout graze like hogs
on September alfalfa

a subterranean world of sunken campfires
where I sit before black ashes
and drink lakewater from a rusted cup
while the sun falls and drives the fish
upward to explode into night

silver gods leaping to swallow the moon.

Culture

So Aeneas walked up the Tiber until he found
a sow
she had a litter of thirty pigs
and he knew it was a sign
that would be the place

Where'd he go to get a boar?

No, it was a myth.

But where'd he get his boar?

He didn't. He killed the sow on the site
and sacrificed
her to the gods for marking the place

You goddam stupid sonofabitch how come you telling me stories like
that I'm busy I haven't got no time to listen to that horseshit you go
get in your car and go on home and find you another book to read
and you tell him next time call me I'll make it right with god and him
both you tell him a sow hog has thirty pigs I'll trade him my pickup
straight acrost sight unseen but I don't want to hear it now I got work
to do who wrote that damn book he must of lived in New York City
his whole life in a whorehouse somewhere just go on I ain't listening
to no more writing like that I don't need it you tell him if he doesn't
know nothing about pigs then don't write about pigs he should find
something else that's all

Nighthunting with John

Last night I went hunting
hogfeed with John
up and down the black alleys
splitting a case of Lucky
looking for the good spots
unburned barrels where expensive folks
pile their scraps for John's sows—
the same as you'n me eat onliest more often
he sez a dozen times
between stops before he sez shit
and turns off his lights
and slips his beat up truck quiet
down the backside of West 5th
where he used to live.

Gotta watch them damn sorry folks
he sez they leave the best stuff
and then wait in the dark so you don't get it
and you better get down in the seat
and he stops and I get down and drink beer
and listen while he sorts through their trash quiet
putting the edibles in the truck bed
along with anything else that looks good
and he gets in and slams the door
and honks and drives off fast
and scrapes the barrels with his beat up truck
and all the lights in the house come on

and he laughs and drinks beer
and sez that's enough let's go
last time I come and banged the cans
those bastards tried to shoot holes in my tires.

The Real Estate

FOR HERBERT SCOTT

Has them real estate been bothering you?
sez John I sed no John
not that I know of John sez
he been after me
ever since they opened that gravels pit
down by my pig pens
he calls up he sez is this John Sims?
I wondered who the hell he thought I'd be
he called up my number
but I sez yas he sez well this is
the real estate and I love to list up
your pig pens for sale
cause I done have it sold for you

I sed what'd you say John?
John sez I sez no that's whar
my pigs is if I sold my pig pens
them pigs wouldn't have no place to be
the real estate he sez well John Sims
you could buy another place to put my pigs
he sed he already had a place picked out
so I sez whar? he sez out by Lund
I sez that's twenty-five miles away
he sez but he can make me a good price
I sez it isn't no water out there
and I ain't hauling no fucking water
he sez but it isn't no water at my pig pens
I sez to him them's only down the road

I can haul it that far
he sez it isn't any either place
so what's the different? I sez twenty-five miles
down and then back is the different
caint you add? he sez well
John Sims you think about it
cause I done got a buyer for your pig pens
he hung up before I could tell him
I didn't have no time to think
I had to cut hay today

I sed John that's that you don't have to sell
anything you don't want to
he won't bother if you make it clear
John sez he done call me back
three times a week for a month
he sez well John Sims I done took
earnest money on them pig pens
when can you get your hogs moved?
I sez I told you twicet already no
this week how come you keep calling me?
he sez them gravels need that land
to park his truck on
I sez my pigs lives there he sez
well John Sims I done took care of that
he told that one at Lund I sez yas
I'd buy that piece of ground there
without no water to build pig pens
twenty-five miles from my house on
I sed John don't let him do that
don't sign anything he can't make
you sell anything you don't want to

John sez they done done this before
it was this aunt my cousin had
that lived in Oklahoma
she had this farm the real estate wanted

to make a graveyard out of
because it was next door
and got full but she sez no
they call her up all the time sez
Mizrez Scott we done got to have that farm
for the graveyard but she wouldn't sell
so they quit except after that
she'd hear all this noise at night
scratch on her winders
and it was dogshit in a sack
on her porch on fire
she'd get it on her shoes
stomping the fire out
she called the sheriff he sez well
Mizrez Scott you taken and buy
you a shotgun for it but you
don't go outside or he can sue you
it has to be breaking in

   two years she set up night
   with that shotgun
   she'd hear noise at the winder she'd
   shoot it and the insurance sed he wouldn't help
   it was costing her eighty dollars a month
   to shoot her winders
   oncet it was the milkcow
   she shot out its eye
   it didn't die but she sed
   it dried up and she had to sell it
   at the auction anyway

   two years after one night
   she never heard nothing she sed
   she seen something outside
   so she shot the winder out
   a little later it was this knock
   on the door so she opened it up

this man standing there shot
she hadn't saw before
blood all down his shirt
he wasn't dead he sez
how come you shot? I ain't scratched
the winder yet you posta wait
till I scratch then shoot
she had to drive him to the hospital
to get them buckshots took out
his shoulder and he told the sheriff
the real estate done paid him
to scratch her winder to scare her off
but the real estate sez they couldn't prove it
they had to let him go
Mizrez Scott was eighty then

I sez that's too bad John sez
she died after that and the real estate
got the county to take the farm
he bought it from the county
and then sold half of it back to them
for twicet what he'd paid them
for the graveyard and kept the rest
cause he was on the commission
I sez that's too bad John
there ought to be laws for that

John sez I caint haul no water
twenty-five miles I'm gone have to buy
that piece of ground next to my place
to put my pigs on
I sed why John? you don't have to sell
your pig pens John sez
I called the gravels man last week
he sez go to hell the real estate
he given me four fousand dollars
for my pig pens and sed he'd help me

move the pigs to a new place
I can buy that piece next door
that has water for that
what am I posta do then?

I didn't say anything so John sed
I caint have the real estate paying no man
two years to scratch on my winders
so I can shoot them out
I have to sleep at night
so I can cut hay in the daytime
wouldn't you? and I nodded yes
because John was right
for that price I would have sold
John's pig pens too

Fall

This day when I see white moon
through a dry branch of another fall at my window,
my fingers stretch to the fire by Kolob
raking and sifting the lifeless ash body,
I rise toward the door drawing crisp wind and
yellow grass in large draughts.

This day I leave her body,
stiff with sleep, in the warm house
to climb toward pale aspen canyons
behind my house. Gasping for breath
I see old initials my father left,
hold my face against cool white bark.

And I return to my ten acres
with its pigs, ripe corn, Jan, still asleep,
aspen powder on my collar, chokecherry-etched
breath, blood streaked in the lines of my hands.

Jan's Birthday

I saved seventy dollars to buy Jan a present
this time because I forgot last year
and went to town to see what I could find.
I found John and he bought a round
and I bought a round and John sez
let's go watch the auction and we drank another beer
and got in my truck and bought a sixpack
and went. They ran a pureblood
spotted poland china sow in and John sez
that's a good one and the man sez who'll start this
at thirty and I felt good about remembering
Jan's birthday and said I will and he started
auctioning but nobody bid and John sez
hope she makes you a nice hog Dave
and I told the man upstairs about Jan's
birthday while he made out the ticket
but he didnt hear and John sez give her to Jan
and she cost sixty-four dollars and ninety-six cents
and after the beer I had thirty-eight cents left
when we loaded up that spotted sow.

I was mad and John sez give her to Jan Dave again
and he bought another beer and I drove
my truck to Woolworth's and went in with my beer
in my hand and bought thirty-eight cents
worth of red ribbon and the lady tied a bow
and gave me a piece of paper so I wrote
For Jan, With Love and John held the spotted sow

by the leg and I tied the ribbon with the bow
around her neck while the lady watched
and said oh my god over and over
the sow screaming like hell stopping cars
and the sheriff drove up and said we had to move
because we were impeding traffic so I pinned the note
to the ribbon and said you gonna help me?
and John sez no I got work to do but you
been to college you'll think of something
so I drove John to his truck
stole two of his beers got drunk
and hit a Piute Indian who hit me back
and a man called the sheriff who sez goddam Dave
and he sez I gotta get out of town or he'll arrest me
and I say Ira I can't drive I'm drunk and Jan will kill me
because it's her birthday and Ira said goddam Dave again
made me sit in the back with the hog
and a deputy named Melvin drove his car to my house
behind us with the red light flashing
while Ira drove me and Jan's seventy-dollar
happy birthday present home.

Shoveling Rolled Barley

got this job selling trailerhouses
he couldn't do that neither
he'd run off all the customers
when they'd come on the lot
they'd look at this trailerhouse he'd say
you sure you can ford something like that?
mebbe you'd better go look at them ones
on the other side the lot
they more for people like you
it don't cost so much over there
you think it's enough grain here
to fill up them other three self feeders?
it better be I caint buy no more
so he went out this one time
set up this trailerhouse they'd solt
he was posta get it levelled
and this other guy he'd hook up the plumbing
Ellis Britton he didn't make no balance
in the middle he's just trying
to do it with the screwerup thingamajig
up on the tongue on the front
he's benting the trailerhouse frame
it wouldn't level
he'd screw it up and go look
the bubble would go one way
he'd go unscrew it back down and look
the bubble would be on the other end
he done it twice or three times

he got mad he taken his hammer
started beating on the front of the trailerhouse
looked like it'd been shot
with a cannonful of ball bearings
all them little dents
that other guy who was there working
sez ohmygod Ellis Britton
what you doing?
Ellis Britton he sez
it isn't none of your goddam business
he thrown that hammer down
scrut it up again
but the bubble was off the other way
he set back and screamed
like he's a crazy womern
beat his hands up against the trailerhouse
till they was both bleeding like hell
sez goddam you goddam yousonofabitch
that's enough in that one
let's pull the pickup over to the one
in that pen it's almost empty
he's so mad he went over got his torch
he lit it and burnt a hole in the end
of the trailerhouse he sez there by god
how'd you like that? so grapt
that screwerup turnt it up some more
bubble went to the other end
he had both ends of that trailerhouse
a foot up above the middle
it was all warped they never could fix it
his face went purple like a balloon
his eyes almost come out the sockets
he picked up that torch
cut the tongue right off the trailerhouse
he hadn't put in no levelling blocks
up front that whole thing
come down right on the ground

busted all the winders out the doors
popped open they never could get them shut
he's so mad he cut that screwerup
in three pieces and thrown it over the fence
that other guy's just standing there
it wasn't nothing he could do but watch
it wasn't even no telephone to call his wife
he never sez nothing
with Ellis Britton holding that cutting torch
so when he's done
he flung the torch down he sez
that's it I quit
I caint take this shit no more
he walked all the way back
to the trailerhouse lot by hisself
when he got there they already known
that other guy drove back and told them
what he'd done but he left
before Ellis Britton got there he sez I quit
pay me off right now
they give him his money too
they known what he might do
at night if they didn't
Ellis Britton he could hold up
his end of a grudge purdy good
help me back up to the feeder
don't let me knock it down
it isn't no sense to doing that
it wasn't nothing left for them to do
he'd ruint that trailerhouse for good
they figgered they come out ahead
if he'd just leave and not come back no more

Mean

HELL HATH NO FURY
LIKE A SOW WITH PIGS

1

Pretty soon now I sed and
John nods his head, watching
so I sed I see she's broke the sack
there's water and his head goes up and down
again but he doesn't say anything
so we both stand and watch
John's big white sow back in her shed
while she breathes easy
seven hundred pounds sprawled across yellow straw
finally John sez any time now
and I nod my head this time
he sez yep just any time
but the only thing we can do is watch
so we stand and wait
and watch John's white sow labor
and John lights a cigarette
to help the time go by while we watch

2

Last time sez John she went craziern hell
I had her in that pen with a wood floor
I put in a lamp for the cold and
she's half done and got up that mean sonofabitch
she done went over and bit that lectric wire
and it shocked her or something

she went like a crazy woman to banging
her head on the walls and floor
and hollered like a elephant shot in the butt
with buckshot she tore hell out of that pen
and had two more pigs while she's standing up and
never knew it she acted like she's blind
and couldn't see nothing I had to get
them pigs out with a rake or she'd of stomped
on them all she jerked that rake
right out of my hand twicet I had
to get it back with a stick sos I could get
them pigs out or they'd be dead
I got all but one that she killed
and she finally went over and lain down
to have her pigs again but ever time
one of them I had out squolt she'd jump up
and go crazy again I had to put them pigs
in the front of my pickup all night
to make her be still and that light
never did work after that she ruint it
so I sez how come you keep her John?
she's too big and mean and John
looks at me like I was nuts or something
he sed cause she had twelve pigs and raised
all but one more besides the one she stomped
that's why, wouldn't you? but I didn't
say anything, John's white sow was too mean
for me, I would have sold her to John
if she was mine but she wasn't
she was already John's so I didn't have to

3

John I sez after a while because she wouldn't pig
I'll bet that sow's got a pig stuck breech
and it won't come but John looks over
at his pickup and doesn't say anything

so I say if she does and it doesn't come
it could kill her and all them pigs too
don't you think? but he keeps looking at
his pickup so I say I don't know of course
but that might be it she's been in labor
a long time and she broke her water
before I got here I saw the last of the wet
when I came but I don't know she's not my sow
it might not be that but John sez real low
she throwed Carl out of the pen that time
he got in and tried to climb out after him
she'd of killed him if she'd got to him
so I decided I wouldn't say anything else
she was John's sow and he'd know what to do

4

Why don't you get in there and look
sez John you know more about that than I do
and I sez no I don't John and I have
to be getting home pretty soon Jan will be
getting worried and I hate to keep
her up John sez Dave I'll give you twenty-five
dollars if you'll go get that pig out and
I sez John I'm not getting in that pen with
that sow for a hundred dollars John sez
okay fifteen dollars cash I sez no John
I'm not going to get in there for a thousand
dollars John sez I'll give you a pig
I sez I wouldn't do it for the sow and all
the pigs loaded up to take to the auction
John sez okay a live pig and you can pick it
but I sed no and I meant it
not for all his pigs and I acted like I
was getting ready to leave

I wasn't I wanted to see how it came out
but I wasn't getting in that pen
so John goddammed me and sed I was a sissy
and I didn't say anything because John was right

5

John sez if I get in there will you come
and hold the lantern in the door so I can see?
and I sed yas because the sow was in
bad shape by then we could see that and
she had to have help but I sed John
if she comes after me I'm getting out
and I'm not going to worry about the lantern
getting out with me so it may get busted
John sez if she gets up you just make sure
you don't get in my way or she'll get you
and the lantern both and I sed okay
because I knew there's no way John
can get out of that pen before me
I wasn't worried about that
so I sed where's the lantern? John sez
over here so we go to his pickup
for the lantern and John gives me the lantern
and some clean rags to hold then
he gets in his jockey box and pulls out
a pistol I sez what's that? and John sez
it's a gun and I sez ohIsee and he sez
I aint getting in there with her without no
gun my mama didn't raise no idiots
and if I need this I want to have it
with me that's why and he put it in
his coat pocket and I didn't say anything
because it wasn't my sow she was John's

6

John climbed in the pen and I followed
he went in the shed with the sow but I
stayed in the door while he moved around
behind her slow to see what she'd do
she had her eyes closed and breathed
hard because she hurt so bad
and I shined the light in so John could see
John knelt down behind her and touched her
but she didn't move so he rolled up his sleeve
and started in to see what was wrong
breech? I whispered and he nodded so
I was right and John went in to try and get it out
John whispers hold still I caint see
and I sez who? and he sez you and
I saw the lantern was shaking I was scared
so I held it with both hands and it
was still John twisted his hand inside the sow
and he sed I got it I'm gone take it out now
he started pulling his arm back and the
pig came out and it was breech
got it? I sed and John sez yas gimme a rag
and I leaned in to hand him a towel and
the pig wiggled in his hand John tried to grab
its mouth but the pig squealed in his hand

7

Goddam you John screamed
the white sow jumped up and bellowed
so loud the tin roof on the shed shook
and jerked around toward John
I stood there like Lot's wife shining the light in
John screams goddam you again
and jumps back against the back wall
of the shed and hits it so hard it should have

come down holding the pig tight against his chest
the sow roars at him the muscles
in her body standing out all the hair on
her back straight up and I think drop that pig
John but I can't say anything I'm frozen
holding the lantern in the door
the sow roaring and John screaming
then he tears at his pocket and pulls out
the pistol goddam you he yells you get away from me
you sonofabitch and the sow barks loud like a maddog
the size of a jersey cow
John points the pistol at her head and it shakes
like an aspen limb in springtime
goddam you and she screams again
snick snick snick snick snick snick snick
I see the empty cylinder turn as John pulls
the trigger and I taste powder in my mouth
drop it! I hear somebody say
John keeps pulling the trigger yelling goddam you
the sow roars and her shoulders bunch up in a knot
she's so mad she's slobbering
DROP IT I yell again and John looks at me
his eyes wide as hubcaps
DROP THAT PIG I scream and I see John's
hand loosen and the pig falls to the ground
but he keeps pulling the trigger snicksnicksnick
the pig hits on its back and lays there
and the sow lowers her head and looks at it
but keeps on grunting loud and mean and fast
John stops pulling the trigger but keeps the pistol
pointed at her head and the pig gets up
and starts moving the sow quits grunting and
sniffs it then looks at John and barks again
John pulls the trigger again but he can't
say anything anymore and the sow turns and lays down
and grunts and another pig pops out
the first pig finds her and tries to find a teat

and the second pig squirms and shakes its head and
tries to clear its nose and John stands with
the pistol pointed at the sow and I stand
holding the lantern and the sow grunts to her pigs
just like we're not there and nothing happened
and I say John? and John points the pistol at me
I say get out John and he sez whar?
and I say get out of that shed John before
she gets up and John sez who? and I say
get out of there John and John looks at the sow
and points the pistol at her and he starts
sliding around the wall and we get out
of John's mean white sow's pen

8

John's shaking so hard he can't light
a cigarette so I do it but he drops it on
the floorboard and I pick it up and put it
in his mouth and he smokes
I say you got a beer? and he sez in the back
I think so I take the lantern and look
and he has some hid in his junk in the bed
I get it and for a long time we drink beer
and don't say anything and I see that my hands
are shaking so the beer foams out the top of my can
so I drink three fast so it won't
and I don't know if he ever finished his
finally I sed John I wouldn't have a pig like that
I'd get rid of her if she's mine she's just too mean
she's gonna kill somebody someday
John's staring straight ahead through the window
the muscles in his face still tight, drawn
he sez goddammit that's too bad
and I sed well you can't help it some go mean
he sez she was a good sow I sez she's okay now
John sez but it was her or me and I sez it's okay

he sips his beer then sets it on the dashboard
and leans back and I see tears in his eyes and
he's still staring straight ahead through the windshield
she was a good sow he sez even if she was mean
goddammit I hated having to shoot her like that
and I looked out the window and didn't
say anything. She was John's sow, not mine.

A Day of Mourning,
24 November 75

I had to sell my black sow Blackula today.
She has become fallow, rejects the boar,
has no pigs and eats too much to keep.
Alas, goddammit. I loved that pig.

Friday Afternoon, Feeding Pigs

John I sed this guy told me
if you broke your leg and fell down
in a pig pen and couldn't get out
the pigs would eat you
do you believe that? John sez
he don't raise no pigs
the one that sed that story
did he? and I sed noIdon'tthinkso
John sez most of the people who sez
things like that don't or is womern
that need something to say
those who do leave it alone

when I's young Eugene Cummings
fell down in his pig pen
and had a heart attackt
he's dead
so when they found him
it was afternoon
he'd gone out to feed his pigs that morning
his face was blue
when they turned him over
to ast him if he was alive or not
his eyes pooched out so
they made dents in the ground
where he lain
they sed you could of sawed them off
with a hack saw

my brother was there he sed
R.B. McCravey he sez he'd of loved
to known what it was Eugene Cummings
was thinking about
that brung it on they sed
he chased around the young girls a lot
with his pickup truck in the evenings
mebbe he was daydreaming
seen a naked vision and couldn't
handle it I wasn't there
so I don't know I's too young back then
when Mama found out
she went over to Mizrez Cumming's house
to help out with the crying
she's a neighbor so she could
make her feel better and find out
whatall happened
how come his eyes was stuck out that way
she took me and I set in the corner
I was only about nine back then
listening and the womern talked it out
Mizrez Cummings she never sed nothing
everbody knew they never slept
in the same bed at night
and hadn't for years she didn't care much
but had to act proper

one of them it was Mavis Tittle I think sed
it was a great issue of blood
that rose up and hit his brains
like a giant hail ball come down from God
and struct his mind with power
he never felt a thing
I think she's lying the way they sez
his eyeballs was out he felt it
they all rocked in the furniture
and nodded to make her feel better

about only having to make up one bed
in the morning any more
it was a bowl of red incarnations
on the table I remember somebody sent
that was pretty but Mizrez Cummings
she wouldn't look at them
I could tell she didn't want
to think about it that much

they buried him and I seen him
in his box at the funeral
you couldn't tell his eyes was pooched out
Rufus got them right
so he just looked dead
his family set together
his boy's girlfriend set by him
she worn this pointed bassiere
that made her look like she had
snow cone cups under there
my brother he kept sighting across
the aisle at her
since it was a funeral
nobody paid him any attention
everbody else was looking at the family
or her too like you do then
to see how they're taking it

it was a new preacher at the churchhouse
he never seen Eugene Cummings before
but he lain it on
sez God he's calling in his folds
preacher talk we couldn't hardly understand
like they learn to do in preacher school
he went on for a hour
about God and heaven and the churchhouse
how glorious Eugene Cummings was
now he's dead in his box

Mama sed one or twice she wondered
if Mizrez Cummings would of liked
to of slipped up and seen who Rufus put
in that box the way that preacher
carried on but she never
I remember I's having a hard time
setting still that long
my brother he had a crick in his neck
the next day from looking across the aisle
at Eugene Cumming's boy's girlfriend's pointed bassiere
for such a time
Mama sed that young feller
he had his wick up so high
he sooted his chimley
but it finally got done and we left

at the graveyard we all shaken hands
after it was over
you'd go through the line and at the end
it was Rufus because he was in charge
him and the preacher
so my brother when he got up to him
he sez Rufus tell me something
did them hogs eat on him any?
Rufus sed not a bite
I heard it because I was right behind
my brother not a bite? he sez
Rufus sed nope not a mark on him
the preacher he had to say something too
so he sez the Lord carries on or somesuch
it never made any sense
but my brother didn't want to be polite
he didn't tell him so
we shaken his hands and just left
he didn't ask Rufus how he got them eyes
mashed back in and I was too young to
so I never did find out

funeral people can do most anything
to a dead body they say and preachers
but you can tell your friend
it don't always happen that way
because Eugene Cummings lain there
the whole day and it was August
so it would of been hot
they'd of smelt him for sure
but his hogs never ate a bite of him
they just set in their mud and watched
cause Rufus sed so at the graveyard
and that's a fact

Dusk

In the snow yesterday's tracks deepen.
A flock of starlings cross my window and break
the monotony of the sky. A last leaf falls,
crosses the yard in front of me, scuttles
over the crust toward the sow's pen,
makes small tattered prints. Nothing better to do
I pull on my heavy jacket and cap and go to chase it down,
a gift for Jan. The red sow pauses and lifts her head
from the trough as I pass.

Oblivious of where I am I wade the snow to the fence.
Wind fills my eyes with frozen leaves, an etched forest
in my blurred vision of night.

A gust bounces against my body. Steps away I see the leaf
on a smooth patch of snow. I pick it up,
then toss it into the north currents. It drifts
beyond my fence like a small animal, fleeing,
worlds twisting away behind like breath. I look away,
to the west, find night already there.

Building a Farrowing Pen

Hot sez John godamitey it's hot
we better drink a coldbeer
and set in the shade a minute
I sed okay cause it was hot
and I was tired of building pigpens
so I went to the pickup and
got the beers while John
found a cool place to sit
where the breeze could cross us
John's stomach hurt where they'd cut
nine feet of amoebic dysentery out
he held himself
arms crossed in front
eyes closed, rocking
I sed hurt? but he didn't answer
rocked and worked his jaw
eyes tight

I was in Misippi John sez finally
we's stringing wore for the lectric
when I seen these wild dogs
people'd turn loose in the sloughs
running in this pack
when I seen them they's just standing there
watching me up on the pole
and I seen them watching
it wasn't nothing else to do but work

and watch out there alone sos I did
it helped the time pass

then they hired on Coy Stribling
Brother Coy Stribling but I wouldn't call him that
his eyes was so close together
he's almost looking out the same hole
he's the Churchofgodofholyanddivineprophesyandrevelation
but it didn't matter they had to fire him
after about a week
he just couldn't catch on to nothing
he wasn't my brother
I couldn't stand it when he looked at me
cause of them eyes

one day it was this deer
run out in a clearing and his leg
was dragging back so I known
them dogs seen him if I did
here they come and drug him down
right out there in front of us
we set there and watched
it standing right there alive
a minute ago
he wasn't no more than down
them wild dogs torn open his guts
and back legs eating it

Coy Stribling he sidled me
he sez Brother John
he called everbody Brother something
whatall his name was
had his little red Gideon newtestament
they give his kids in the school
he kept in his pocket
out in his hand
he sez that there's a vision sent down from God Amitey

I almost sez oh bullshit Coy Stribling
it's dogs people turned loose
trying to find something to eat to
stay alive but I didn't
you caint do nothing for people like that
it's too late
with his eyes like that he needed
something to believe in
so I let it alone
he was standing and nodding his head
almost slobbering he believed it so

that deer raised his head
and looked back over his shoulder
watched them wild dogs eat it
saw pieces of his own belly tore off
and swallered and them wild dogs go back
for more me standing
out there a hundred yards off watching
it was like how a sow hog
when she's farreling hurts like a sonofabitch
getting them babies out her stomach
but she'll turn her head up
to look at them while she's doing it
you can see that same look
in her eyes and
it just lain its head down
and died
I was watching

Coy Stribling he never seen a thing
after them wild dogs took him down
he's talking to hisself and nodding
at his newtestament in his hand
it wasn't nothing else he could do

I set my beer on the ground
between my legs and saw the foam rise
John didn't say anything else
he lit a cigarette and smoked and
we sat in the shade and let the wind
blow over us while we rested
John's arms crossed in front
his head back against the pigpen
eyes up to the scraps of cloud
drifting north, rocking

The Farm

We sold it. To a man
who would be a patriarch.
I told John we were closed in,
subdivisions and trailers all around,
complaints of the smell (though
there was none), Ira came out
and told me to keep them fenced
(though none broke out), the neighbors
frightened because someone's cousin's
friend heard of a hog
that ate a child who fell in the pen (though
their children rode my sows
at feeding time), because I was tired,
because Jan carried our child and could
no longer help, because she wanted a home.

And the patriarch lost his first crop
to weeds, threw a rod in the tractor,
dug a basement and moved the trailer on
for extra bedrooms, cut the water lines
for a ditch, subdivided the farm
and sold the pigs for sausage. I told John
they were his, they were no longer mine,
I couldn't be responsible.

The wire connecting our voices was silent
for a moment. "You stupid sonofabitch," was all
he finally said. "You poor stupid bastard."

Aftermath

There were pigs
in the night, a wild herd
overran the farm, trampled
my fences and flowers, rooted the garden,
lost in the depths of overturned garbage cans
their grunts echo the darkness
as they search the land
while the night reaches out before them
like a starving child.

Jan nudged me awake
to the walls of this new place we call
home. "It's all right," she said
and slept. And I lay awake
the rest of the night, listening
as the wind carried the scraps of sound,
bounced them against the house,
muffled grunts of the abandoned herd
searching us out in the night.

Baalam

All the way from Twin Falls
Fred came to help out while Jan had
her surgery and Willa took care of the kid
and I and Fred we chopped wood
played cribbage and fixed up the house
while Jan got well. And then we went to
town to find an ax handle and we found
John and a case of beer and we all went
to John's pig pens to see if that old ax handle
he had was out there

2

There was this man sez Fred
up to Hailey who drove all the way to
Missouri to buy these walking horses
and John sez isatso and Fred sez he paid
a hell of a price and John sez he was in
Missouri once and they raise good hogs there
and Fred sez he bought two mares one stud and a
gelding he didn't know why he bought the gelding
and brought them back to Idaho and John
sez that's too far to haul hogs he wouldn't
do that and the stud, Fred sez, keeps breaking
fence and then goes after the gelding
and finally that man he's had enough

so he ropes the stud and throws him and
castrates him right then and there
by god that stopped that and John sez
boars generally leave barrows alone
you can leave them in the same pen and Fred
sez he never got a colt out of that stud
all that money wasted

3

John sez he had a ewe that kept breaking
fence and Fred sez onct a animal starts
it's hard to stop and John sez one day he had it
so he got a length of hose and chased her
and Fred sez his brother was good with a black
snake and used it on bulls and John sez he
caught her and whipped her good till her ears bled
and she jumped back in and Fred's brother
could tick a fly off a horse's ear and that ewe
lambed that night but Al Fred's brother could
lay one open he whipped hell out of that black
English bull one day and John sez somebody
shoulda whipped him because that ewe and her
lamb both died but Al never hit a man with
a whip so John shouldn't ask him he'd have to find
somebody else

4

And I told about Wesley Steven's proud cut
stud back in Texas and John sez he was there
once and he saw a damn big hog farm there
and Fred sez what's proud cut and John sez
whoever cut that horse never got the squealer
and that horse shoots blanks but he keeps
shooting and Fred sez isatso? and John sez yas
he seen a boar that was castrated proud

and he bred any sow that would stand
but she wouldn't pig and Fred sez so that's the
squealer and I sez Wesley Steven's stud
mounted a mare but she wasn't ready and John
sez that's what they'll do they ain't got no
sense and they hurry too much and Fred sez
he knew a man onct that way and he's in
prison and I sez that mare laid back
her ears and kicked that stud's belly open
and John sez that's the good thing about hogs
they don't kick and Fred sez that sonofabitch
got sentenced to forty years and I sez Wesley
had to kill the stud because he was ruptured so
bad and John sez his proud cut boar died
of the blood poison and Fred sez that ain't
a long enough sentence for rape they oughta
gut shoot the bastard and I just thought
that poor son of a bitch, that poor sonofabitch

5

That same feller from Hailey
who castrated his stud sez Fred was out
walking and he saw a doe and fawn
and John sez he didn't see even one
goddam deer the whole hunting season and I
sez I didn't even go and Fred sez the
doe jumped the fence but the fawn couldn't
and John sez his big white sow's got to
fence jumping and he can't hold her
in and I sez he oughta get a
electric fence and he sez he'll maybe
ring her nose or chop it with a butcher knife
that'll by god do it and the guy runs up
and grabs the fawn and tries to cut its throat
and John sez even that don't always work so I
say why not? and he sez it'll stop rooting

but not jumping and Fred sez that fawn
stomped the piss out of the guy and put
bruises all over him and got away
and John knew a man that got stepped on
by a circus elephant and it broke his foot and
I sez that hurts (I know I broke my foot and
it hurt like hell) but John sed he never
felt it but he walks with a cane
and that guy fell in a ditch on the way
home and broke his leg and when they found
him he was crawling and he kept saying
where'd that little fucker go?

6

John found the ax handle but it wouldn't
work so we drank beer and I started to tell
about balling a collie dog when I was fourteen
but didn't besides it wasn't me it was Kenneth
Bullard and it wasn't a dog but a cow and
he stood on a box and she shit his pants full
down around his ankles but I wasn't even
there I just heard and John talked about farming
and Fred talked about Idaho and I got drunk
and went off by myself and didn't say anything but just
kept thinking about all them hogs
that used to be mine, all mine.

Epilogue

WHAT MIGHT HAVE BEEN AND WHAT HAS BEEN
POINT TO ONE END, WHICH IS ALWAYS PRESENT.
  "Burnt Norton"

IN MY BEGINNING IS MY END.
IN MY END IS MY BEGINNING.
  "East Coker"
    T. S. Eliot

Months begat seasons begat a year
another
begat a child, another
begat all the successes: advancement,
rank, salary equal to almost one-
half the yearly inflation,
begat respectability, political acumen

voted for all the losers,
Ananias Frogeyes elected, reelected, scholarly insight
studied the use of feminine endings in Milton
by the book, rocked no boats
therefore *was* happy, indeed, passive

Jan made it official,
asked: are you happy?
replied: of course. Why not?
asked: are you sure?
replied: I'm very busy. Do you need something?

And on Saturday Jan left
for groceries, I babysat
studied scientific humanism, read essays
she returned, honked
honked, honked

until I came outside, passive
said get this sonbitch unloaded
replied: I beg your pardon
said either get it unloaded
or go back and set on your butt

I'll do it

Saw in the pickup bed
fence wire, twenty cedar posts, sheet iron,
one dozen 2x6 boards, a gunny sack
behold, a gunny sack, *tow sack*
tied with a strand of wire
bailing wore I've seen that before
a voice whispered, where have you been,
Jan? Jan where have you . . .
tow sack while I watched
                              moved

And I *known*
I known whatalls in that towsack's
trouble, break any fence
any man can build or fix
lay in mud, dig holes
belly up to the sun, eat
anything can be eat, gnaw
whatall'll hold still to be gnawed
piss me off worsen anything alive
bring out all the worse
all the best
                    in me

behind the spare tire another sack
behold squirmed
tow sack moved, rolled, tow sack
squealed, squirmed, rooted, tow sack
tied with bailing wore grunted

but it caint holt it long
don't worry about being polite
you got to hurry
it'll get out goddam
                    another one

David Lee is currently Chairman of the
Department of Language and Literature at
Southern Utah State College in Cedar City. He
has received several fellowships from the
National Endowment for the Humanities and
from the National Endowment for the Arts. His
publications include *The Porcine Legacy*
(Copper Canyon Press, 1978), *Driving and
Drinking* (Copper Canyon Press, 1979, 1982),
Shadow Weaver (Brooding Heron Press, 1984),
and *The Porcine Canticles* (Copper Canyon
Press, 1984). *Day's Work* was awarded the
Publication prize of the Utah Original Writing
Competition.

Printed in the USA
CPSIA information can be obtained
at www.ICGtesting.com
JSHW082221140824
68134JS00015B/663